**W9-CBU-180**

INSIDE ELECTIONS

# VOTERS

FROM

PRIMARIES

to

DECISION NIGHT

ROBERT GRAYSON

LERNER PUBLICATIONS ◆ MINNEAPOLIS

Lerner Publications Company
A division of Lerner Publishing Group, Inc.
241 First Avenue North
Minneapolis, MN 55401 USA

For reading levels and more information, look up this title at www.lernerbooks.com.

Main body text set in Calvert MT Std Light 10/16.
Typeface provided by Monotype Typography.

**Library of Congress Cataloging-in-Publication Data**

Grayson, Robert, 1951–
   Voters : from primaries to decision night / by Robert Grayson.
      pages cm. — (Inside elections)
   Includes bibliographical references.
   ISBN 978-1-4677-7911-1 (lb : alk. paper) — ISBN 978-1-4677-8529-7
(pb : alk. paper) — ISBN 978-1-4677-8530-3 (eb pdf)
   1. Elections—United States—Juvenile literature.  2. Voting—United
States—Juvenile literature.  I. Title.
   JK1978.G73  2016
   324.973—dc23                                    2015000948

Manufactured in the United States of America
1 – VP – 7/15/15

# CONTENTS

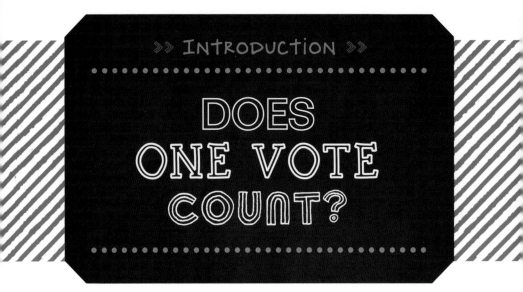

# DOES ONE VOTE COUNT?

It's the first Tuesday in November. You notice a few people—teachers, neighbors, your friend's dad—wearing I Voted stickers. Did you remember that today was Election Day? Maybe you'll be walking around with a sticker like that in a few years. Or maybe you've heard that voting doesn't really matter. You might have even heard adults say that the system is rigged.

The US election system certainly isn't free of problems. Voting can be inconvenient and confusing. Supporters of a candidate or a political party sometimes even try to make it difficult for opponents' supporters to vote at all.

But in the United States, voting is a right guaranteed by the Constitution. Many people also think of it as an honor and a responsibility. By voting, a US citizen does more than simply cast a ballot for a few government leaders. Voting lets people voice their concerns and take a stand on issues. It allows them to support candidates whom they believe will best represent their views and goals.

Many citizens take great pride in voting. This voter wears an I Voted sticker after casting his ballot on Election Day.

Roughly 180 million people are registered voters in the United States. Your relatives, neighbors, and teachers may be among them. But you probably know some people who are eligible to vote yet don't actually do it. They may believe a single vote doesn't make much difference. Hundreds of thousands—even millions—of votes can be cast in an election. With that many voters, how much can a single vote matter?

Consider the 2008 national election. Slightly more than 2.9 million people voted in the Minnesota race for US Senate. When all the votes were added up, Republican Norman Coleman lost his Senate seat to Democratic challenger Al Franken by just 312 votes. That's just one example of how even a handful of votes can determine the outcome of an election and set the tone for future laws and policies.

So what does it really mean to be a voter in a US election? Voters can participate at various steps of the election process, from volunteering for candidates during campaign season to casting their ballots on Election Day. A voter's job isn't always easy or clear, but it's hugely important in a democratic society.

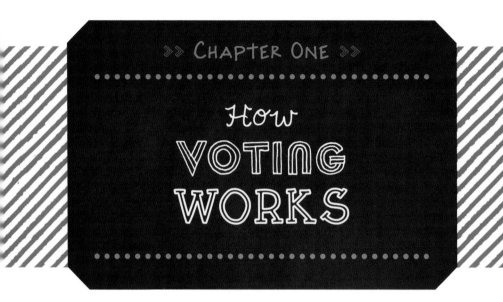

# CHAPTER ONE

# How VOTING WORKS

Representatives are a very important part of the US government. Each year, thousands of new laws go into effect around the country. Those laws start out as bills that have to be debated and voted on. It would be impossible for every citizen to vote on every piece of legislation that is proposed on the federal, state, or local level.

In a democracy like the United States, voters elect representatives to serve in public office, and those representatives pass laws that citizens must follow. Even if a voter didn't support the winning candidate, that candidate is still responsible for representing the voter's interests. And the winner in a close election has to pay particular attention to the concerns of the opposition to try to win those people's support in future elections.

## WHO CAN VOTE?

In the early days of US democracy, only white men over the age of twenty-one who owned a certain amount of land could vote.

# HISTORY OF VOTING RIGHTS IN THE UNITED STATES

1770
1780
1790
1800
1810
1820
1830
1840
1850
1860
1870
1880
1890
1900
1910
1920
1930
1940
1950
1960
1970
1980
1990
2000

**1787:** White men over twenty-one who own property can vote.

**Early 1800s:** Many states allow all white men to vote, whether or not they own property.

**1870:** the Fifteenth Amendment guarantees African American men the right to vote.

**1920:** the Nineteenth Amendment guarantees women the right to vote.

**1924:** The Indian Citizenship Act makes all American Indians US citizens (and eligible to vote).

**1943:** The Magnuson Immigration Act allows people of Chinese descent to become US citizens.

**1952:** The Immigration and Nationality Act of 1952 allows all people of Asian descent to become citizens.

**1965:** The Voting Rights Act guarantees voting rights to all racial minorities.

**1971:** the Twenty-Sixth Amendment lowers the voting age to eighteen.

So what about women, African Americans, American Indians, and white men without enough property? They were out of luck.

Over the years, these groups and others won the legal right to vote. Laws were put in place to protect every citizen's voting rights. This was a long, hard-fought process. In some forms, it continues into the twenty-first century.

In a modern US election, people who meet these requirements are eligible to vote:

1. **Be a US citizen.** Anyone born in the United States is automatically a citizen. So is anyone with a parent who is a US citizen. People from other countries can become US citizens if they have lived in the United States for five years and go through a long, complex application and testing process.

2. **Be at least eighteen years old.** In some states, a person can vote in a primary election or a caucus if he or she is seventeen but will turn eighteen before the general election.

3. **Be registered to vote.** It's not enough to be eligible to vote. People have to be registered, and their registration has to be up to date.

## REGISTERING TO VOTE

In some countries, the government automatically registers people to vote when they reach a certain age or when they become citizens. In the United States, registration isn't quite that easy. US citizens have to fill out registration forms—usually several weeks before Election Day.

Government workers process the registration forms, and the information becomes part of official records called voter rolls. The goal is to prevent people from committing voter fraud: voting more than once in an election, voting in place of someone else, or voting in an area where they don't actually live.

People can register at some government offices, including motor vehicle departments and social service agencies. Or people can pick up registration forms at registration drives or print them off the Internet. Then, in most states, they can mail completed forms to the government office that processes them. Some states even allow online registration. A voter has to register only once, unless he or she moves or changes his or her name. Then the voter has to fill out a new registration form.

Each state has its own requirements to register to vote. For instance, in most states, a person must live in a precinct—the area where he or she will vote—for at least thirty days before Election Day to cast a ballot. People who are overseas for jobs, military service, or school are exceptions to this rule if they have a permanent US residence. Homeless people often have a hard time registering to vote, but by law, they're allowed to list shelters, parks, or street corners as residences.

## Voter Registration or Voter Suppression?

The purpose of voter registration laws is to keep track of voters and prevent voter fraud. But voter registration has also been misused to make voting difficult or even impossible for certain groups of people, such as American Indians, African Americans, and people with low incomes. At various times in US history, laws have required people to pass tests or pay fees before they could register to vote. This was partly due to prejudice. It was also partly because certain groups of people tended to support a certain party, and the other party wanted to prevent those groups from voting. For instance, immediately after the Civil War (1861–1865), African American voters in the South elected many Republican legislators who supported their civil rights. Some white Democrats worked to decrease African American voter registration so that Democrats had a better chance of winning elections in the South. Through a series of constitutional amendments, laws, and court decisions, many of these abuses were eventually outlawed.

As part of the registration process in some states, voters are asked to declare a party affiliation. There are two major political parties in the United States: the Democratic Party and the Republican Party. Voters can register as members of either party. They can also choose not to label themselves as either one and register as independents. Choosing a party on a registration form doesn't mean these voters have to vote for members of that party in an election. But this choice does affect which primaries or caucuses a person can vote in.

## VOTER ID LAWS

Some states have laws that require voters to show identification before they are allowed to vote on Election Day. As of early 2015, voter ID laws were in effect in thirty states. Sixteen of those states specifically require a photo ID, such as a driver's license.

Supporters claim that voter ID laws help prevent voter fraud at the polls. But opponents say voter fraud is extremely rare. They point to a study done on voter fraud in the United States between 2002 and 2007. The report cited only 120 cases of voter fraud nationwide over that five-year period. No one knows whether other cases of fraud go unreported. Backers of voter ID laws say yes, and opponents say probably not.

Opponents of voter ID laws also argue that the laws make it difficult for many elderly and low-income citizens to register. Getting copies of birth certificates, marriage licenses, or other documents needed to meet voter ID requirements can be time-consuming and costly. Drivers' licenses cost up to sixty dollars. Some states offer a free ID option, but this still requires proof of identity, usually in the form of a birth certificate. Copies of birth certificates can cost up to twenty-five dollars. Critics of voter ID laws say that's more than many people can afford. As a result, eligible citizens may not register to vote.

Voter ID laws in various states have been challenged in court with different outcomes. In 2008, for instance, the US Supreme Court upheld Indiana's voter ID law, finding it caused no undue burden to voters. But in October 2014, the Supreme Court blocked Wisconsin's voter identification law from taking effect, saying that the law needed further review.

## OPPOSING VIEWPOINTS: ON PROGRESS IN VOTING RIGHTS

**PRO**

"Nobody will ever deprive the American people of the right to vote except the American people themselves—and the only way they could do this is by not voting at all."
—President Franklin D. Roosevelt, October 5, 1944

**CON**

"All types of conniving methods are still being used to prevent [people] from becoming registered voters. The denial of this sacred right is a tragic betrayal of . . . our democratic traditions, and it is democracy turned upside down."
—Martin Luther King Jr., civil rights activist, May 17, 1957

## SAME-DAY REGISTRATION

Imagine your family just moved. With so much else on their minds—registering you at a new school, setting up the Internet service and garbage collection, figuring out where to buy groceries—the adults in your family forgot to register to vote at your new address. They missed the voter registration deadline, so they can't vote in the upcoming election.

In some states, situations like this aren't a problem for would-be voters. Election Day Registration, or Same-Day Registration (SDR), allows voters with the proper identification to sign up to vote on Election Day. SDR rules vary from state to state. In some districts, voters can register right at the polling place. In other districts, they may have to visit the local registrar's office first. Thirteen states allow SDR. So does the nation's capital, Washington, DC. In states with SDR, voter turnout is about 10 percent higher, on average, than in states without this option.

Opponents of SDR claim it's too expensive and complicated to set up in more populated states. Extra poll workers have to be hired and trained to handle the registration process on Election Day. And government staff must put in more time to enter voters' information into the permanent voter rolls. The cost of paying all those employees adds up. California, with a population of 38.3 million, would have to spend roughly $6 million a year to create an SDR program. Supporters of Same-Day Registration say the cost is only a small fraction of election costs. And they insist that making voting easier is worth the price tag.

## WHAT DO PEOPLE VOTE FOR?

Once a person is registered to vote, he or she can go to the local polling place on Election Day and cast a ballot. Polling places are usually located in public places such as schools,

# SAME-DAY REGISTRATION (SDR)

## PROS:

- States with SDR have higher voter turnout.

- SDR gives all eligible voters a chance to vote, including people who have recently moved or changed their names and haven't had time to update their registration.

- States with SDR have some of the toughest identification requirements in place to prevent voter fraud.

## CONS:

- SDR increases the cost of elections because trained personnel need to be on-site to register voters at every polling place.

- SDR can create lines at polling places, causing some voters to leave in frustration without casting a ballot.

- Opponents believe SDR increases the possibility of voter fraud.

recreation centers, and government buildings. Citizens have a chance to visit a polling place every November. Of course, presidential elections happen only once every four years. But citizens elect representatives at other levels of government, from the smallest local offices to the US Congress, at various times.

The US electoral system is divided into units, each with its own level of government. Voters elect representatives within each unit.

1. **A voting precinct is one section of a town or a city.** Precincts don't have their own elected governments, but they do have election officials who oversee voting procedures in the area. Most voters cast their ballots at polling places in the precincts where they live.

2. **A ward is made up of several precincts.** Voters elect an alderman or a council member to represent their ward on a city or municipal council.

3. **A municipality (a city or a town) contains several wards.** Voters in many municipalities elect mayors and school board members.

4. **A county includes several municipalities.** Voters elect county judges, a county sheriff, and many other county officials.

5. **A district covers a much larger geographical area.** A single district can include many counties. Voters in each district elect state legislators, who make laws for their state. They also elect a member of the US House of Representatives, who helps make laws for the entire nation. There are different districts for state elections and federal elections. State legislators represent smaller districts than federal representatives do.

A voter registration drive gives people a chance to fill out registration forms on the spot. Then the organizers of the drive deliver the forms to a government office for processing.

Citizens can also vote for candidates at the state level. Every four years, people in each state elect a governor, who works with the state legislature to run the state government. Every six years, voters elect two US senators, who represent their state in Congress. At the national level, all voters can choose the president and vice president of the United States every four years.

In municipal, county, and state elections, people may vote for or against ballot measures, also called propositions. These are specific questions and issues that voters approve or reject directly. If approved by a majority of voters, a ballot measure will become a law. In many states, voters themselves propose certain kinds of measures. If enough people sign a petition, they can get their measure added to the next election's ballot.

## VOTING BLOCS

Election officials and politicians pay a lot of attention to voter registration. By examining lists of registered voters for a particular area, they can see how many men and women are registered, the age range of voters in a particular area, and which party has the most voters registered. This gives politicians a sense of how much support they or their party will likely get in this area.

That way, candidates can decide where to focus their efforts. And they can craft messages and set up voter outreach efforts that aim to influence certain groups of voters, or voting blocs, in an area. For instance, if a lot of young people are registered in Candidate X's district, Candidate X might focus on issues important to many young people, such as job creation and making education more affordable.

But gender, age, and party affiliation aren't the only factors that make up voting blocs. These are just the groups that can be tracked through voter registration records. Other voting blocs can include people of a particular ethnic group, race,

Women make up a large and important voting bloc in the United States. Issues such as abortion and equal pay directly affect many women. Politicians trying to appeal to women voters may focus on these issues.

or income level. Information like this isn't usually included on voter registration lists, but politicians can find it elsewhere and can consider it as they plan their campaigns.

Plenty of information about voters is available to politicians and their supporters. But a person's actual vote is secret. People do not have to reveal how they voted.

## WHY VOTES COUNT

Voters' choices can make an impact that lasts for generations. When elected candidates take office, they make laws and policies that affect people's everyday lives. Imagine how different the nation's history would have been if Abraham Lincoln hadn't been elected president in 1860. After all, his election sparked the Civil War and led to the end of legalized slavery in the United States. Or what if Franklin D. Roosevelt had lost the 1936 election? Would another president have outlawed child labor? Probably, eventually—but it happened in 1938 partly because voters had elected Roosevelt. Decisions like these still affect your daily life. Recent presidential policies may affect the lives of your children and grandchildren.

And that's just presidential elections. Consider the laws your state legislature deals with—laws about education, public health, same-sex marriage, taxes, and so much more. Then think about your local government. Have your school board members approved the budget for your school's athletic programs so you can play on a sports team? Is there a fine for playing music too loudly after dark? Elected officials are responsible for all those policies and many, many others. And voters are responsible for the elected officials. They're also often responsible for directly changing laws and policies by voting on ballot measures. Voters may not know how their votes will affect the future. But it's safe to say everyone's vote does count.

# CHAPTER TWO

# PRIMARIES, CAUCUSES, and CONVENTIONS

L ong before Election Day rolls around, voters can help decide whose names will appear on the ballot. That's especially true for major races—elections for the presidency, a governorship, or a seat in the US Congress. Presidential hopefuls may decide to make a run for the White House years before the actual election. But many of them won't make it to the finish line. Voters narrow down the field through a system of primaries and caucuses that decides each party's nominees.

## WHAT ARE PRIMARIES AND CAUCUSES?

Primaries are preliminary elections within a specific party to choose who will compete in the general election. Voters go to their usual polling places to cast ballots for a party's candidates for national, state, and local offices. There are several different types of primaries, and parties in each state choose which type to use.

   **Closed primaries.** Only voters who are registered as members of the party can vote. Only registered Republicans can vote in a Republican primary, and the same is true for Democrats. Independent voters can't participate unless they reregister as Democrats or Republicans.

**Semi-closed primaries.** Registered party members can vote only in their party's primary. But independent voters can vote in whichever primary they choose.

**Open primaries.** A voter doesn't have to be a member of a political party to vote in that party's primary. But voters do have to choose to vote in either the Democratic or the Republican primary. So a registered Democrat could choose to vote in the Republican primary—just not in both parties' primaries.

Open primaries can have an extra element of surprise, because people may vote in a party's primary even if they don't support that party. Those voters don't necessarily want this party's strongest candidate to win. In fact, they may want the opposite. For example, in 2014 Eric Cantor, a member of the US House of Representatives, unexpectedly lost the Republican primary in his home state of Virginia. Democratic voters may have voted for his opponent, Dave Brat, in the open primary. They may have thought Brat was a more controversial candidate and that a Democratic candidate could more easily defeat him in the general election. This practice of the opposite party basically sabotaging a primary is called raiding, or party crashing.

Some states have caucuses instead of primaries. A caucus is a large meeting of political party members. Voters attend caucuses in their precincts to discuss candidates and issues. Then they decide whom to support for party nominations. These meetings last several hours and almost always involve some debates and deal making. Since primaries take less time and are less complicated, a vast majority of states use the primary system instead of caucuses.

# OPEN PRIMARIES IN PRESIDENTIAL ELECTIONS

## PROS:

- Open primaries get independent voters involved in the nominating process.

- Open primaries usually result in the selection of moderate candidates with broader appeal, instead of those with extreme views.

- Open primaries favor the wishes of voters over party leaders' interests.

## CONS:

- Open primaries give voters less incentive to join a political party, which means they're less likely to be active in politics—and less likely to even vote at all.

- Open primaries may allow voters to select a candidate whose views differ from those of the party faithful.

- People from the opposing party may deliberately select a weak candidate, giving their own party a better chance of winning the general election.

# THE PRIMARY SEASON SCHEDULE

Unlike general elections, presidential primaries and caucuses are not all held on the same day. In fact, many are held weeks apart. In the year of a presidential election, primaries and caucuses usually start in January or February and continue through June. Iowa is the first state to hold a caucus in a presidential election year. New Hampshire is the first state to hold a primary.

Because of this staggering, voters in states with early primaries and caucuses have a lot of power. They're the ones who pick the early favorites in the race. So candidates tend to focus on those states, trying to make a good impression on these voters.

Some presidential candidates start organizing their primary campaigns as much as a year and a half before primary season. Their goal is to become familiar to voters and to start gathering support as soon as possible. Support for this stage of a campaign comes in two main forms: donations and volunteers.

Candidates try to develop grassroots organizations made up of dedicated supporters. These people don't just plan to vote for a candidate. They plan to convince as many other people as possible to vote for that candidate too. Volunteers may go door-to-door passing out campaign materials and telling people about a candidate. Campaign staff and volunteers also send e-mails, make phone calls, create a social media presence for the candidate, and organize rallies to build enthusiasm ahead of a primary.

Meanwhile, the candidates themselves spend a lot of time in states with early primaries and caucuses. Voters there have many chances to see presidential hopefuls in person. They also deal with a lot of media attention, calls and e-mails from campaigns, political ads, and opinion pollsters asking how

## Super Tuesday

During presidential election years, some states hold primaries and caucuses on the same day, called Super Tuesday. Hundreds of delegates to the Democratic and Republican conventions are up for grabs. Voters in those states can solidify the momentum a candidate picked up in Iowa or New Hampshire. Or they can give a trailing candidate a major boost.

Super Tuesday takes place early in the primary season, in either late February or early March. The number of states holding primaries and caucuses that day varies, and so does the number of delegates at stake. Seven states scheduled elections for March 1, 2016. Florida, Massachusetts, Texas, and Virginia were among the Super Tuesday primary holders.

they plan to vote. For some citizens, it's an exciting time. For others, the experience is draining. If voters feel too pestered by a candidate's campaign or dislike a candidate's ads, that candidate may not fare well in the primary.

So candidates try very hard to make a positive impression on these early voters. A candidate who wins the support of Iowa's and New Hampshire's voters often becomes a front-runner—even if he or she seemed like a long shot before. The candidate receives increased media coverage, which can capture more voters' interest. An early primary victory adds momentum to a campaign. And by contrast, candidates who lose badly in the first few primaries usually drop out of the race. Some never make it past New Hampshire.

This system frustrates many people in states with later primaries and caucuses. Some voters feel that by the time they cast their ballots, the race has already been decided. But if more than one candidate has a strong showing early on, later primaries become crucial. This happened in the 2008 primary season, when Hillary Clinton and Barack Obama faced off for the Democratic presidential nomination. Both candidates snagged early victories and were more or less neck and neck for months. It took until March for Obama to gain a sizable lead with wins in Texas, Wyoming, and Mississippi. And he still didn't net enough votes to secure the party nomination until June.

## THE VOTER DECIDES

Voters in primary elections can press candidates for answers about their goals and plans. They must pay close attention to candidates' statements and their records on the issues. That way, voters can decide which candidate is the best qualified to represent the party in the general election.

Many states hold presidential debates during primary season. These are forums where candidates discuss issues face-to-face. Viewers can judge for themselves which of the candidates is the most knowledgeable about the issues—and who has the most appealing personality. There are separate debates for each party, where all the candidates running for president in that party present their views. Candidates know that what matters most in these debates is how voters see them. The voters decide who wins a debate based on how convincing and likable they find each candidate.

What makes primaries and caucuses different from general elections? They involve battles within the parties themselves. In each party, several candidates may be running in a primary or a caucus. And these candidates may share very similar political views. Voters may find that no one candidate's ideas or proposals stand out from the rest. That turns the primary

Democrat Barack Obama was a little-known US senator from Illinois when he entered the presidential race in 2008. His campaign worked hard to help voters become familiar with him during primary season.

election into more of a popularity contest. It may come down to one candidate's appearance or personality appealing to the voters more than another's.

## DELEGATES TO THE CONVENTIONS

After each primary and caucus win, a presidential candidate is awarded a certain number of delegates. Delegates are voters who will attend the party's national convention, a big meeting of party leaders. There, the delegates will vote for and eventually nominate a presidential candidate. They also nominate a vice presidential candidate, whom the presidential nominee has picked ahead of time. The presidential and vice presidential candidates run as a team, or a ticket, and their names appear on the ballot together.

Presidential candidates in each party need a specific number of delegates to win the nomination. The number varies in both national parties. For example, to win the Republican presidential nomination in 2012, a candidate needed 1,144 delegates.

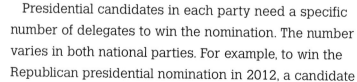

Each state has a different number of delegates, based on rules developed by each national party. Some states have winner-take-all primaries. In those states, the candidate who wins the party's presidential primary automatically wins *all* the party delegates. Other states use a proportional system. If a candidate gets 27 percent of the votes in a proportional primary, that person will also get 27 percent of the delegates.

Most states have binding primaries. That means the delegates that a candidate wins during a primary have to vote for that candidate at the national convention. A few states hold nonbinding primaries, in which a candidate's delegates do *not* have to vote for that person at the convention, but they usually do. There are also binding and nonbinding caucuses.

## Power to the People

In modern elections, voters play a key role in the nomination process. But it wasn't always that way. During the nation's early years, members of Congress selected the candidates for president. That's how John Adams, the country's second president, was chosen as a candidate in 1796.

In 1832 political parties started using national conventions to nominate presidential candidates. Delegates from each state attended these national party conventions. But the delegates were chosen by party leaders, not by voters. And those delegates nominated whichever candidates the party leaders favored. That didn't start to change until the early twentieth century, when the first presidential primaries were held. These primaries let voters choose convention delegates, not the presidential candidates themselves. During the 1910s, states finally began holding primaries with candidates' names on the ballots.

In a close race, it's possible that none of the candidates will win enough delegates to secure the party nomination. If that happens, candidates have to make deals with one another to try to get enough votes. For instance, Candidate A might agree to put Candidate B on the ticket as vice president in exchange for Candidate B's delegates. Often candidates who drop out of the race "release" their delegates to vote for the leading candidate. But candidates can also hold onto their delegates all the way up to the convention.

The result is a brokered convention, with delegates voting several times—and deal making happening behind the scenes—until one candidate gets a majority of delegate votes. In 2008 some analysts predicted that this could happen with

At the 2012 Republican National Convention, presidential candidate Mitt Romney addressed a crowd of supportive delegates.

the Democratic presidential nomination. But Barack Obama won enough delegates to clinch the nomination. Hillary Clinton then dropped out of the race and released her delegates to vote for him at the convention.

Besides selecting candidates for president and vice president, convention delegates decide on the party's platform. The platform is a statement of values and goals that party members share. Party members want candidates to stand by the platform in the general election.

The Democratic and Republican National Conventions are basically giant rallies. They usually run for four days. Voters can watch the main events on TV at home. Conventions are supposed to get people excited about the candidates. But some voters use these occasions to voice their criticism of a party. Protests outside convention centers are common. For instance, the 2008 Republican National Convention in Saint Paul, Minnesota, drew ten thousand protesters who opposed Republican policies. But whether conventions spark enthusiasm or anger, they remind voters of the choices they'll face in the upcoming election.

# CHAPTER THREE

# The CAMPAIGN and THE VOTERS

After a national convention, a presidential nominee of either party usually sees an increase in popularity. This "bounce" comes from the excitement surrounding the nomination and convention. The upswing in public opinion will eventually level off, though, and candidates focus on winning over enough voters to gain a victory in November.

Candidates have already worked to win over voters from their own party. But in the general election, those aren't the only voters who count. Candidates must also try to lure voters from the opposing party to their camp. They need independent voters to support them too. That's why campaigns launch voter outreach efforts on a larger scale as Election Day approaches.

During campaign season, voters consider candidates for all levels of public office. They want to know who shares their values and goals. They also try to figure out which candidates will actually do their job well and fulfill their campaign promises once elected.

During election season, campaign workers and volunteers often knock on doors and talk to voters in person about candidates or issues.

## CAMPAIGN OUTREACH

The primary and caucus season gives candidates a chance to set up strong campaign organizations in some areas. These grassroots groups work to win voter support in the run-up to the general election. They're made up of hired staff members and volunteers—ordinary voters hoping to rally their fellow voters to the candidate's cause.

Presidential candidates want strong campaign organizations in as many states as possible so that voters can get to know them. It would be hard for the presidential or vice presidential candidate to spend equal time in every state during the general election campaign. Instead, they often concentrate on states where the election seems close or on states where they *need* to win to carry the election. So in states the candidates don't visit or visit only rarely, it's up to campaign staff to engage voters. That means organizing rallies and debate-viewing parties, contacting voters through e-mails and phone calls, and door-knocking to ask people in person for their support.

Staff and volunteers for major campaigns try to target these efforts. They want their messages to address the specific concerns of the people in their area. Voters may be paying attention to big issues, such as the nation's overall economy, but they're also interested in matters closer to home, such as the job market in their city. Campaign organizations aim to be familiar with the local hot-button topics. That way they can answer voters' questions about a candidate's stance on particular issues.

## OPINION POLLS

Opinion polls can tell candidates how they're doing with voters so far. Pollsters question various voting blocs in different voting districts to gauge how well a campaign is doing. Based on this information, many polls can guess the likely outcome of the election if it were held on the day the poll is taken.

Campaign coordinators use polls to figure out how their candidates are faring with the party faithful, as well as with independent and undecided voters. Independent and undecided voters may tell pollsters which candidate they favor at the moment, even though they may not end up casting a vote for that person. This tells campaign staff whether the candidate is making any inroads with these voting blocs. Based on information from the polls, they may revise the campaign strategy to try to be more appealing to voters.

News organizations and political researchers frequently organize public polls of likely voters. Candidates' campaign organizations can also conduct polls, called internal polls. Internal polls often point out specific areas where a candidate is weak and needs to work harder to win votes. For instance, Candidate Y might not have much support from Latino voters due to his stance on immigration laws. Or Candidate W might not be popular with blue-collar workers because she doesn't talk about job creation.

Polls can provide good news too. They might show that a candidate is putting together a strong coalition of voters from different backgrounds. That's the kind of backing a candidate needs to win in the general election.

But even the most reliable polls can be wrong. No one can predict exactly what voters will do on Election Day. So even if the polls show their candidate with a sizable lead, campaign staff and volunteers still work hard to get the vote out, because anything can happen—and often does.

## INDEPENDENT AND UNDECIDED VOTERS

The big wild cards in any general election, especially a national one, are independent and undecided voters. These voters can swing a close election in favor of one candidate or another.

Displaying campaign signs is one way for voters to voice support for a candidate, a party, or a cause.

## Voting for Third Parties

Most voters identify with either the Republican or Democratic Party. But plenty of people around the country feel that neither party represents their views. Some political activists, usually united by a particular issue, may form a smaller third party. One of the largest third parties in the United States is the Libertarian Party, whose members describe themselves as strongly against government oversight. Another well-known third party is the Green Party, which focuses on ecological issues. A third party can nominate its own candidates for president and vice president. No third-party candidate has yet won a presidential election in the United States. But if enough people vote for a third-party candidate, their votes do leave a mark. In the 2000 presidential election, for instance, the Green Party nominated Ralph Nader. Nader got about 2.7 percent of the popular vote nationwide. In Florida, he won 97,488 votes. Some analysts believe that if those people had voted for Democratic candidate Al Gore, Gore would have won the election. Instead, he lost to Republican George W. Bush by a very slim margin.

Candidates, campaign staff, and volunteers have to work especially hard to get the support of these voters.

The independent vote is up for grabs in every election. Since independents don't belong to any party, their voting habits are more flexible than those of die-hard party members. They're less likely to vote for Candidate X just because she has her party's endorsement. Instead, they tend to base their votes on specific issues and their impressions of Candidate X as an individual.

It's hard to pinpoint exactly how many independent voters there are in the United States because the number keeps changing dramatically. Some surveys show that as many as 42 percent of registered voters consider themselves independents. Many of these people may lean toward one

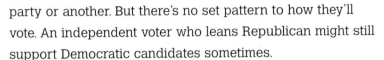

party or another. But there's no set pattern to how they'll vote. An independent voter who leans Republican might still support Democratic candidates sometimes.

Undecided voters may be independents. They may also be members of a political party who are not solidly behind their party's candidate. That means they might cross party lines and vote for the opposing candidate. In any case, they haven't made up their minds yet.

Some voters stay undecided right up to Election Day. Others lean toward a candidate but have doubts. An undecided voter might like Candidate Z's plans for helping small businesses but disagree with his position on same-sex marriage. That voter will have to weigh these issues and decide which matters more. A voter might support a candidate's platform but dislike his personality—or like a candidate personally but hate her ideas. Maybe the voter dislikes *both* candidates equally. Whatever their reasons for being undecided, citizens in this camp are willing to consider more than one option. And that gives every candidate a reason to reach out to them.

## VOTER ENGAGEMENT

It's up to voters to challenge candidates on the issues. Citizens must make the candidates aware of their concerns, especially if they think candidates aren't addressing those matters. Informed voters play a vital role in the electoral system. These voters ask the toughest questions. They push the candidates and their campaigns for direct, thoughtful answers. Voters who are familiar with the issues and demand thorough responses from the candidates make the system work.

# CHAPTER FOUR

# The ELECTORAL COLLEGE

It takes more than winning the popular vote to get elected president of the United States. In the 2000 presidential election, for example, Democrat Al Gore received roughly 540,000 more votes than his Republican opponent, George W. Bush. But Gore lost the election. How could that happen?

Gore had failed to win a majority of votes in the Electoral College. This is the system used to elect the president and vice president of the United States. In each state, when people cast a ballot for the presidential ticket of their choice, they're actually voting for a group of electors. Think of electors as super-voters. Much like delegates at party conventions, they're pledged to vote for specific candidates. And they'll eventually be the ones to officially choose the president and vice president.

## WHAT IS THE ELECTORAL COLLEGE?

You may be thinking, "Wait a minute. I thought elections were decided directly by ordinary voters, not by special super-voters." That's true, except when it comes to presidential elections. This is because the nation's founders developed a complicated, roundabout system for electing the president and vice president.

When the framers of the US Constitution developed this system in 1787, the United States had only thirteen states. The population was scattered, and communication was slow and unreliable. Many people couldn't read, and those who could didn't have easy access to information. They couldn't research a candidate on the Internet or tune in to live news coverage of a campaign. And without modern transportation systems, it wasn't easy for candidates to travel and meet voters face-to-face either.

## 2012 ELECTORAL COLLEGE VOTE

WA 12
OR 7
ID 4
MT 3
ND 3
MN 10
VT 3
ME 4
NH 4
NV 6
UT 6
WY 3
SD 3
WI 10
MI 16
NY 29
MA 11
RI 4
CA 55
CO 9
NE 5
IA 6
IL 20
IN 11
OH 18
PA 20
CT 7
NJ 14
DE 3
AZ 11
KS 6
MO 10
WV 5
VA 13
MD 10
NM 5
OK 7
AR 6
KY 8
TN 11
NC 15
SC 9
TX 38
MS 6
AL 9
GA 16
LA 8
FL 29
AK 3
HI 4

OBAMA

ROMNEY

Many of the Constitution's framers feared that a direct election, better known as an election by popular vote, was impractical. These leaders assumed people wouldn't be able to make informed decisions and would tend to vote for candidates from their home states—that is, people they were familiar with. If it came down to a popularity contest, candidates from more heavily populated states would be almost guaranteed to win. Smaller, less populated states would never have a chance to get a candidate elected.

One alternative would have been to let the members of Congress choose the president. But many leaders felt that would put too much power in the hands of the government's legislative branch. So a compromise was struck.

The people would vote for president—but through a system of electors. Citizens in each state would choose their own slate of electors. Those electors would then vote for the president.

James Madison, one of the framers of the US Constitution, wanted presidential elections to be decided by popular vote. Others disagreed, so Madison supported a compromise: the Electoral College.

Technically anyone who isn't a member of the US Congress can be an elector, but in the country's early years, electors tended to be better educated than average US citizens. This gave government leaders confidence that electors would cast informed votes. Still, most voters felt the electors representing their state would vote for the presidential candidate that the majority of people in the state supported. In theory, the system was a win-win solution.

## HOW DOES THE ELECTORAL COLLEGE WORK?

A candidate for president still needs a majority of the nation's electoral votes to win the election. If no candidate gets a majority, the House of Representatives can decide the election. The modern Electoral College is made up of 538 electors, based on the number of representatives each state has in the US Congress. It works like this:

**100 ELECTORS**, to match the number of US senators (two for each state)

**+ 435 ELECTORS**, to match the number of members of the House of Representatives (divided up based on each state's population)

**+ 3 ELECTORS** for Washington, DC

**= 538 MEMBERS OF THE ELECTORAL COLLEGE**

A candidate must win a majority—at least 270—of these electoral votes to be elected president.

A heavily populated state like California has fifty-three members in the House of Representatives plus two US senators. That gives the state fifty-five electoral votes. Nebraska, on the other hand, has a much smaller population and gets only three seats in the House. With its two US senators added in, Nebraska has just five electoral votes.

The electors in every state all cast their ballots on the same day, but that takes place well after the November general election. The electors gather in their own states on the Monday following the second Wednesday in December. (The rule that electors must meet in their own states was originally meant to prevent all the members of the Electoral College from getting together in one place and making deals.)

Each state's electors generally vote for the candidate who won their state's popular vote. Some states have laws that require electors to do that. Once in a while, an elector breaks with tradition and votes for a candidate other than the one who captured a state's popular vote. But this has never changed the election's outcome. After the electors vote, their votes are sealed and sent to the president of the US Senate. The Senate president reads the results to both houses of Congress on January 6.

## CRITICISMS OF THE ELECTORAL COLLEGE

Many people believe that the Electoral College is out of date and no longer serves the country's needs. Critics of the system want to reform it or get rid of it completely. But it would take a constitutional amendment to abolish the Electoral College, and constitutional amendments are very rare.

A major criticism of the Electoral College is that it can skew election results. A candidate can get the most total votes—including plenty of votes in states where he doesn't get a majority—but still lose the Electoral College vote. In 2000, for example, Al Gore won the overall popular vote for the presidency. But George Bush narrowly beat him in electoral votes, which made him the victor. Many people were outraged that Bush became president despite losing the popular vote.

## PRESIDENTIAL ELECTIONS DECIDED BY THE ELECTORAL COLLEGE VOTE

| VOTE | CANDIDATES | WINNER OF THE POPULAR VOTE | WINNER BY ELECTORAL COLLEGE |
|------|-----------|----------------------------|-----------------------------|
| 1876 | Rutherford B. Hayes (Republican) vs. Samuel J. Tilden (Democrat) | Tilden, by 255,000 votes | Hayes, by 1 vote |
| 1888 | Grover Cleveland (Democrat) vs. Benjamin Harrison (Republican) | Cleveland, by 110,000 votes | Harrison, by 65 votes |
| 2000 | George W. Bush (Republican) vs. Al Gore (Democrat) | Gore, by 540,000 votes | Bush, by 5 votes |

Another complaint is that the Electoral College encourages presidential candidates to focus their campaigns on the states with the most electoral votes. Candidates know which states they have to carry to win the presidency. They can even win these states by razor-thin margins, because in forty-eight of the fifty states the electoral votes are awarded on a winner-take-all basis. So racking up impressive popular vote totals in heavily populated states doesn't affect the candidate's electoral votes.

Two states, Maine and Nebraska, split their electoral votes instead of using the winner-take-all method. In this system, two electors are awarded to the candidate who wins the statewide popular vote. The remaining electors are divided among whichever candidates win the popular vote in each of the state's congressional districts. So if Candidate B wins in a district but not the whole state, she still gets an electoral vote. But as of 2015, neither Nebraska nor Maine has ever split its electoral vote, because the statewide winner of the popular vote has also won the popular vote in each district.

## PROS:

- The system is part of the nation's history and democratic tradition.

- The system gives small states a real voice in the election.

- Residents of one geographical area can't decide the election because no region has enough votes to give one candidate a majority.

## CONS:

- The system is outdated and comes from a time when most average voters knew little about candidates outside of their area.

- Many people's votes don't fully count, because the candidate who wins the popular vote does not necessarily win the election.

- The system gives too much power to swing states. Candidates have little incentive to campaign in states they already know they are likely to win or lose.

US senator Cory Booker (*center*) and congressional candidate Aimee Belgard (*left*), both New Jersey Democrats, make phone calls to voters before the 2014 midterm elections.

## RED STATES VS. BLUE STATES

In certain states, people tend to vote a particular way. The overall vote is so predictable that these states are identified as red states (Republican strongholds) and blue states (Democratic strongholds). For instance, Texas is a well-known red state, and California is a die-hard blue state. A purple state is a swing state, also called a battleground state. This is a state where no political party has overwhelming support. So the popular vote for president, along with that state's electoral votes, can go either way from election to election. Swing states often hold the key to a presidential election's outcome. As a result, candidates spend a lot of time and money in those states, trying to attract voters.

There's no question that the Electoral College plays a major role in presidential elections. But winning the popular vote in each state is vital to winning that state's electors. That means everyone's vote still counts.

# CHAPTER FIVE

# ELECTION DAY PROMISES and PROBLEMS

Election Day can signal a new direction for the nation, as well as for many states and smaller communities. For candidates, campaign workers, and volunteers, it's the longest day of the political season. But it's also about the voters making democracy work.

## WORKING THE POLLS

At some point on Election Day, voters head to their polling places. Some voters show up even before the polls open. Those are the poll workers—people who are either paid by the municipal government or are volunteering their time to keep the voting process running smoothly. They've been trained to help voters cast their ballots. Poll workers have several important tasks on Election Day.

1. **Arrive early to set up.** Poll workers set up voting equipment and check that it is working properly. They also organize copies of the voter rolls, an alphabetized list of registered voters for the precinct. And they may put up signs in and around the

building to help voters find the polling place.

2. **Open the polling place.** Voting hours vary from state to state. Polling places usually open between six and nine o'clock in the morning and close between six and nine o'clock at night, local time. Most states try to keep polling places open for about twelve hours on Election Day.

3. **Maintain order and oversee voting.** Poll workers check that everyone who shows up to cast a ballot is registered in the precinct or district. In some states, this is as simple as asking for each person's name and address, then comparing that information to what's listed in the voter rolls. In other states, poll workers check voters' IDs. In many areas that allow same-day registration, poll workers can register voters on the spot by checking their documents and guiding them through the necessary paperwork. A big part of a poll worker's job is to keep these processes organized, with orderly and fast-moving lines. Poll workers can show people how to cast their ballots if voters need assistance.

## GETTING OUT THE VOTE

While poll workers are running polling places, other groups are working hard to get as many people to those polling places as possible. Some groups are nonpartisan activist organizations. They don't represent any political party, and they don't try to influence people to vote for specific candidates. They simply want to help the democratic process by making sure that eligible people can and do vote.

Campaign workers and volunteers also make a final push to get people to the polls. But they focus specifically on voters

A person's vote is secret, so polling places provide booths or privacy screens so that voters can mark their choices without anyone else seeing their ballots.

who favor their candidates. After months of campaigning, a candidate can lose simply because supporters didn't go to their polling places and cast a ballot. So throughout Election Day, campaign workers and volunteers contact voters by phone, via e-mail, or through door-knocking, urging them to vote. In states that allow SDR, campaign workers and activists alike may set up registration drives near polling places.

In some countries, voting is mandatory. A total of twenty-six nations, including Australia, Brazil, and Mexico, require their citizens to vote. That's not the case in the United States—and it shows. On average, only 54 percent of eligible voters have voted in presidential elections since 1960. And even fewer vote in elections that don't feature a presidential race. For instance, during the 2012 presidential election, 57.5 percent of eligible voters cast a ballot. But two years later, in the midterm elections, only 36.4 percent of eligible voters turned out.

Voters may sit out an election for any number of reasons. In every election, voter apathy can decrease turnout. Some people simply don't care who wins or loses. They may believe none of the candidates represent their views or care about their needs. Or they may think that a single vote won't make a difference in the results.

Sometimes good news hinders voter participation. If voters see news reports that the candidate they support is expected to win, they might think they don't need to vote. If enough voters feel that way and opt not to cast a ballot, the front-runner might not get enough votes for a victory after all.

Weather affects voter turnout too. Snowstorms and downpours can make it hard for voters to get to their polling places on Election Day, especially if they don't have reliable transportation. And transportation is another big factor in who does and doesn't go to the polls. Elderly voters who no longer drive or voters who don't own cars are especially likely to miss out on voting. A voter's car might also break down, or the ride a voter was waiting for might fail to show up. Many campaigns assign volunteers to drive voters to and from the polls on Election Day.

## LONG LINES, BIGGER PROBLEMS

Another challenge to voter turnout can be the actual voting process. Maybe a member of your family has gone to vote on Election Day only to find a long line at the polls. Long lines aren't uncommon, especially when voter turnout is high. Voters may have to wait longer to vote in precincts that don't have enough poll workers or voting equipment. Lines also tend to form in states that have voter ID laws. Checking IDs, making sure voters are at the right precinct, and helping them figure out where they should be voting if they're in the wrong place can take a long time.

# VOTER ID LAWS

## PROS:

- The laws prevent voter fraud by making it harder for a person to vote using someone else's name.

- The ID required to vote is the same kind of ID required to board a plane or cash a check, and free options are available in sixteen of the seventeen states that use voter ID laws.

- Voter ID laws encourage voters to keep their registration up to date.

## CONS:

- The laws aren't necessary to prevent voter fraud because voter fraud is so rare.

- Many voters don't have an ID that meets their state's specific registration requirements, and many can't afford one.

- Checking voters' IDs leads to longer lines at polling places, which can decrease voter turnout.

Voters in Miami, Florida, wait in line at a polling place on November 6, 2012.

Many people believe these experiences are part of a bigger problem: deliberate attempts to prevent certain votes from being counted. Imagine a race for mayor in the city of Undecided. Most people who live in precincts 2, 3, and 5 are likely to vote for Candidate A. If that happens, Candidate A will win. Supporters of Candidate B might try to prevent those people from casting ballots. Government officials who favor Candidate B could simply set aside less money to pay poll workers and to supply voting equipment to precincts 2, 3, and 5. Voters in those precincts will have a long wait. If they have to return to work, pick up their children from school, or run important errands, some people may leave before they have a chance to vote. Meanwhile, voters in precincts 1 and 4 have plenty of poll workers and equipment. They have no trouble voting. So more people in the city end up voting for Candidate B than for Candidate A.

In the 2012 national elections, some Democrats claimed that this had happened around the country. Lines were especially long in neighborhoods with mostly African American and

Hispanic residents. Traditionally, these voting blocs favor Democratic candidates. Many Democrats were concerned about possible voter suppression. Some people waited more than seven hours to cast their ballots. These events sparked calls for more flexible voting systems that don't involve showing up in person on a single day.

## ABSENTEE VOTING AND EARLY VOTING

Absentee voting is one alternative to traditional in-person voting. Sometimes people know ahead of time that they won't make it to the polling place on Election Day. In every state, these voters can request and cast an absentee ballot. Twenty states allow absentee voting only if the voter has one of these reasons for not coming to the polling place on Election Day:

- The voter will be out of town on Election Day.
- The voter is ill or physically limited and is unable to come out and vote.
- The voter is temporarily living outside the country for work, military service, or school.

Twenty-seven states, plus Washington, DC, allow voters to cast an absentee ballot without giving any specific reason. Each state has varying rules and deadlines for no-excuse absentee voting.

A growing number of states, including California, New Jersey, Arizona, and Utah, permit permanent absentee voting. That means once a voter opts into the program, that person will receive an absentee ballot in the mail for every election, including primaries.

Another take on this method is early voting. In states with early voting, a citizen can vote at a designated voting site during a specific time window before the election, instead of on just a single day. Early voting is permitted in thirty-three states and Washington, DC. Depending on the state, voting can start anywhere from forty-five days to four days before Election Day. Early votes are counted once voting officially ends on Election Day.

## ALL-MAIL VOTING

Three states—Colorado, Oregon, and Washington—conduct all their elections by mail. Registered voters receive a paper ballot in the mail well before an election. In Colorado, for instance, the ballots go out twenty-two days before Election Day. Voters then have a time window in which to cast their ballots. Each voter places a completed ballot in a security envelope and either mails it back to the county clerk's office or drops it off at an official ballot drop box. Ballots must be received by a certain time on Election Day. In Colorado that deadline is seven p.m. All-mail voting is especially convenient in rural communities, where it may be difficult for voters to get to a polling place on one specific day.

Critics have voiced some concerns about all-mail voting, though. The biggest fear is voter fraud. What if Carl fills out Marina's ballot as well as his own? Maybe Marina is ill, uninterested in voting, or no longer living in the precinct. According to critics, it would be easy for Carl to "steal" Marina's vote in any of these cases. As a result, all-mail voting has not spread to other states. Still, very little evidence of any widespread voter fraud has surfaced in the three states that have all-mail voting.

Another concern about all-mail voting is that for a vote to count, a voter must sign the ballot. There have been reports of voters failing to sign their ballots. But this doesn't seem to be a frequent problem.

All-mail elections can both save and cost money. Poll workers are no longer needed. Neither are voting machines. That means big savings. But the equipment to read mail-in ballots accurately is very expensive.

Will this system take hold in other states in the future? That remains to be seen. But for Colorado, Oregon, and Washington, the method seems to work for many citizens. Voter turnout in all three states in the 2012 election was higher than the national average.

## THE FUTURE OF VOTING METHODS

Early voting and all-mail voting aren't the only options for boosting voter turnout. One idea is to hold presidential elections on weekends, giving people two days to cast their ballots, rather than one. Another possibility is online voting. Some countries, such as Canada, already use online voting. But in the United States, this method has gotten little support from election officials, due to concerns about security issues and glitches. So for the time being, most citizens continue to cast their ballots in person. And activists continue to search for ways to make the process easier for voters.

# CHAPTER SIX

# COUNTING the VOTE

In some nations with corrupt governments, it doesn't much matter how many people vote or which candidates they support. The government has already decided who will be declared the winner. Official reports of voting tallies will reflect that decision—whether or not it's the reality. In the United States, voters expect election results to be counted accurately and reported honestly. Fair elections— and respect for the outcomes of those elections—are at the heart of US democracy.

## EXIT POLLS

Unofficial vote counting actually starts during Election Day, while voters are still casting ballots. As voters exit their polling places, they might be approached by exit pollsters. An exit poll is different from an opinion poll. In an opinion poll, taken during the campaign, voters are asked who they are likely to vote for in the election. In an exit poll, voters are asked who they actually cast a vote for and why. They might also be asked which issues are most important to them.

An exit pollster talks to voters immediately after they leave their polling place. Voters are not required to answer an exit pollster's questions. But if they do, they help pollsters and news outlets predict the outcome of the election. Poll results also help show voter trends throughout the country. Experts can study polling results to figure out why a particular candidate won the election. In a presidential election, people are especially interested in which candidate attracted which voting blocs. The reasons people voted a certain way and the types of people who voted in a particular election often influence how public officials govern.

But exit polling has raised concerns, especially in presidential races, because of the nation's different time zones. People are still voting in the Pacific time zone long after polling places in the East have closed. Do results in the presidential elections coming in from the East Coast influence voters out west? That debate has been going on for years.

## VOTE COUNTING GONE WRONG

As soon as a state's polls close, poll workers officially record the vote tallies for their precincts and report the results. At this stage of Election Day, there's more at stake than just determining a winner. Voters must have complete confidence in the methods used to tabulate the results. Otherwise, people may question the accuracy of those results. If voters don't trust the official vote counting, they may doubt that their voices were heard or that voting was worthwhile in the first place. And if citizens don't think their representatives were elected fair and square, they may not trust those officeholders.

In every state, candidates who believe the results of an election are inaccurate can ask for votes to be counted again. A recount can also happen if the election is extremely close, with only a few votes separating the winner and the loser. And if a ballot measure in a county, district, or local election loses by a very slim margin, ordinary voters can file an official request for a recount too.

Recounts became headline news in Florida during the presidential election in 2000. Flaws in the vote-counting methods there left the election undecided for thirty-six days.

In that election, many Florida polling places used punch cards. Voters punched holes in paper ballots next to the names of their chosen candidates. These punch cards were then fed into a computer, which counted the votes. The problem with this technology was that voters had to punch a hole clearly through the card. If any little pieces of cardboard, called chads, were left hanging from the back of the card, the computer might misread the punch card.

The tiny fragments of paper on the back of this punch card are hanging chads. Hanging chads caused inaccurate vote counts in several Florida counties during the 2000 election.

## Stuffing the Ballot Box

Vote counting has always had its controversies. In the nineteenth century, people voted on paper ballots, which they then placed in a locked wooden ballot box. In a close election, losing candidates who thought they should have won often claimed that dishonest people had put extra votes in the ballot collection container. An objective investigation sometimes proved them right.

Both George W. Bush and Al Gore needed to win Florida to win the presidential election. At first, Bush seemed to have carried the state by 1,784 votes. Under Florida law, such a small margin of victory requires a recount. That second count gave Bush a margin of victory of only 327 votes, with some absentee ballots yet to be counted.

Gore exercised his right to have another recount done—this time by hand. That recount focused on four large Florida counties with heavy voter turnout. Workers overseen by a county judge would have to examine and count all the punch cards in the four counties.

The recount raised questions about ballots where chads were not completely removed or were just slightly indented. Was that a valid vote or not? It was uncharted territory for election officials.

Bush and the Republican Party went to court to challenge the recount. The US Supreme Court called a halt to the recount, ruling that it was not being conducted the same way in each of the four counties. In addition, the justices said there wasn't enough time to set up a consistent recount procedure in all four counties by the time the election had to be finalized.

When the count was halted, George Bush won the Florida popular vote by just 537 votes—out of 6 million votes cast in the state. With Florida, Bush had enough Electoral College votes to win the presidential election.

The recount left many people across the country worried or outraged. Could they trust the electoral system? These concerns prompted some major revisions in US voting systems. The focus was on restoring confidence in how votes were counted. In 2002 Congress passed the Help America Vote Act. It provided money to upgrade voting systems throughout the nation.

## MODERN VOTE COUNTING

Since the 2000 election, two main voting systems have been used in elections around the country. More than 50 percent of the nation uses the optical scan paper ballot system. Voters fill in ovals or boxes on paper ballots next to the names of their chosen candidates. The votes are then scanned and counted by a machine called an optical scanning device. This is the same system used to grade standardized tests in schools.

The optical scan system offers both a paper trail and a speedy vote count. On the downside, the scanners can jam. Overall, though, vote counts for optical scan readable ballots are much more accurate than those for punch cards.

The most common alternative to the optical scanner is a computer called a direct recording electronic (DRE) system. Voters cast their ballots on touch screens or push-button terminals. The votes are recorded on the system's memory cartridge, diskette, or smart card. Most DRE systems don't have a paper backup, which makes accurate recounts difficult. Yet supporters claim they are not only reliable but secure, easy to use, and able to provide results fast.

## Mechanical Voting Machines

Mechanical voting machines came into use in the 1890s. People entered a voting booth with a curtain for privacy. Inside the booth was a steel voting machine, which displayed the candidates' names above a series of levers. A voter simply pulled a lever under a candidate's name to vote for that candidate. The machine automatically recorded the vote and reset for the next voter.

When the polls closed, poll workers removed a panel on the voting machine, and a mechanical vote counter showed the vote tallies for each of the candidates. The major problem with this system was that it left no paper trail. Recounts consisted of simply rereading the tallies recorded by the machine. There was no way to know if a machine had recorded a vote incorrectly. The machines also broke down a lot. Mechanical voting machines are no longer used in US elections.

## AND THE WINNER IS . . .

Once citizens have cast their ballots and wrapped up their get-out-the-vote efforts, they wait for the results. Most candidates have a central location or headquarters where campaign workers and volunteers gather on election night. Meanwhile, voters at home can watch live news coverage to follow the results.

In most elections, the news media can accurately announce a winner once votes have been tallied. Then it's time for speeches. Whether a candidate wins or loses, he or she usually comes out and addresses supporters. Often a losing candidate urges supporters to rally behind the winner. Or the loser might vow to keep fighting for supporters' goals and values despite this setback. A winning candidate may congratulate an opponent on a well-run race and briefly outline an agenda for his or her time in office.

Win or lose, candidates thank the voters who backed them. Winners know that without the people who volunteered for their campaigns, engaged with their ideas, and cast their ballots for them, victory would not have been possible. And when the winner reaches the end of his or her term in office, if voters don't believe they've been served well, that winner can easily become the loser of the next race. The final word in any election goes to the voters.

# SOURCE NOTES

11   Franklin Roosevelt, *Public Papers of the Presidents of the United States: F. D. Roosevelt*, 1944–1945, vol. 13 (Place: Publisher, 1950), 86.

11   Martin Luther King Jr., "Give Us the Ballot, We Will Transform the South," *PBS*, accessed February 20, 2015, http://www.pbs.org/pov /pov2008/election/wvote/king.html.

48   John Fund, "Voter Fraud: We've Got Proof It's Easy," *National Review*, January 12, 2014, http://www.nationalreview.com/article/368234 /voter-fraud-weve-got-proof-its-easy-john-fund.

48   Heather K. Gerken, "Make It Easy: The Case for Automatic Registration," *Democracy*, no. 28 (Spring 2013), accessed April 28, 2015, http://www.democracyjournal.org/28/make-it-easy-the-case -for-automatic-registration.php.

# GLOSSARY

**abolish:** to get rid of or outlaw

**affiliation:** membership in or official support of

**apathy:** lack of enthusiasm or interest

**ballot:** an official form that lists the candidates in an election and which voters can mark with their choices

**caucus:** a meeting of political party members for the purpose of choosing candidates or deciding policy

**delegates:** people chosen to act on behalf of others

**democracy:** a political system in which people govern themselves, usually by electing representatives

**eligible:** qualified for and having the right to something

**grassroots:** starting at the community level

**moderate:** a person whose political views are not extreme or radical

**nominee:** a person chosen by a political party to run for an elected office

**nonpartisan:** not supporting any particular political group

**political party:** an organized group of people with similar political views who try to achieve their goals by getting their members elected to public office

**polling place:** a place where people vote

**popular vote:** a process in which citizens vote directly for a candidate, or the total vote tally from that process

**primary:** an election used to select party nominees

**slate:** a group of people running for office together

**voter fraud:** an illegal use of the electoral system by voters, such as voting twice in the same election or voting when not eligible

# SELECTED BIBLIOGRAPHY

Congressional Quarterly. *Presidential Elections, 1789–2004.* Washington, DC: CQ, 2005.

Crotty, William J., and John S. Jackson. *Presidential Primaries and Nominations.* Washington, DC: CQ, 1985.

Faucheux, Ronald A. *Running for Office: The Strategies, Techniques, and Messages Modern Political Candidates Need to Win Elections.* New York: M. Evans, 2002.

Gangale, Thomas. *From the Primaries to the Polls: How to Repair America's Broken Presidential Nomination Process.* Westport, CT: Praeger, 2008.

Gray, Lee Learner. *How We Choose a President: The Election Year.* 5th ed. New York: St. Martin's, 1980.

Griffith, Benjamin E., ed. *America Votes: A Guide to Modern Election Law and Voting Rights.* Chicago: American Bar Association, 2008.

Henningfeld, Diane Andrews, ed. *Should the United States Move to Electronic Voting?* Detroit: Greenhaven, 2008.

Keyssar, Alexander. *The Right to Vote: The Contested History of Democracy in the United States.* New York: Basic Books, 2000.

Tarr, Dave, and Bob Benenson. *Elections A to Z.* 4th ed. Thousand Oaks, CA: CQ, 2012.

"What Is the Electoral College?" *US Electoral College.* Accessed March 2, 2015. http://www.archives.gov/federal-register/electoral-college/about.html

# FURTHER INFORMATION

Congress for Kids—Elections
http://www.congressforkids.net/Elections_index.htm
Learn more about candidates, political parties, and elections in this interactive site just for kids.

Donovan, Sandy. *Media: From News Coverage to Political Advertising*. Minneapolis: Lerner Publications, 2016.
Find out how the media influences voters—and candidates—during election season.

McPherson, Stephanie Sammartino. *Political Parties: From Nominations to Victory Celebrations*. Minneapolis: Lerner Publications, 2016.
Learn about how political parties move from candidate nominations to election night results.

Merino, Noël, ed. *The Election Process*. Detroit: Greenhaven, 2013.
Sink your teeth into more details about the US election process.

OpenSecrets.org Center for Responsive Politics—Learning Center
https://www.opensecrets.org/resources/learn
Dig deeper into election spending and campaign finance with fact sheets, timelines, and answers to frequently asked questions on this website from the Center for Responsive Politics.

Our White House—Race to the Ballot: The Our White House Presidential Campaign and Election Kit for Kids!
http://www.ourwhitehouse.org/campaignandelectionkit.html
Find information, resources, and activities to dig deeper into the topic of presidential elections.

# INDEX

## PHOTO ACKNOWLEDGMENTS

The images in this book are used with the permission of: © iStockphoto. com/cajoer (banners); © iStockphoto.com/jamtoons (arrows), (stars), (speech bubbles); © iStockphoto.com/ginosphotos, (bunting); © iStockphoto.com/Kontrec (chalkboard ); © iStockphoto.com/ OliaFedorovsky (lines); © Blend Images/Hill Street Studios/Getty Images, pp. 5, 44; © Ariel Skelley/Blend Images/Getty Images, p. 15; AP Photo/Jae C. Hong, pp. 16, 26; © Samuel Corum/Anadolu Agency/Getty Images, p. 24; © John Gress/Corbis, p. 29; AP Photo/Phelan M. Ebenhack, p. 31; © Laura Westlund/Independent Picture Service, p. 35; © World History Archive/ Alamy, p. 36; AP Photo/Mel Evans, p. 41; AP Photo/Tim Chapman/The Miami Herald, p. 47.

Front cover: © iStockphoto.com/Kontrec (chalkboard background); © iStockphoto.com/Electric_Crayon (border); © iStockphoto.com/StasKhom (people and capitol); © iStockphoto.com/cajoer (banners); © iStockphoto. com/OliaFedorovsky (patterns); © iStockphoto.com/jamtoons (doodle arrows).

Back cover: © iStockphoto.com/jamtoons (doodle arrows) (stars).